Unaccompanied

Unaccompanied

Javier Zamora

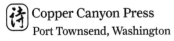 Copper Canyon Press
Port Townsend, Washington

Copyright 2017 by Javier Zamora

Printed in the United States of America

Cover art: Photograph © Tomás Castelazo, www.tomascastelazo.com / Wikimedia Commons / CC BY-SA 4.0

Copper Canyon Press is in residence at Fort Worden State Park in Port Townsend, Washington, under the auspices of Centrum. Centrum is a gathering place for artists and creative thinkers from around the world, students of all ages and backgrounds, and audiences seeking extraordinary cultural enrichment.

LIBRARY OF CONGRESS CATALOGING-IN-PUBLICATION DATA
Names: Zamora, Javier, author.
Title: Unaccompanied / Javier Zamora.
Description: Port Townsend, Washington : Copper Canyon Press, [2017]
Identifiers: LCCN 2017022737 | ISBN 9781556595110 (paperback)
Subjects: | BISAC: POETRY / Caribbean & Latin American.
Classification: LCC PS3626.A62786 A6 2017 | DDC 811/.6—dc23
LC record available at https://lccn.loc.gov/2017022737

Copper Canyon Press
Post Office Box 271
Port Townsend, Washington 98368

www.coppercanyonpress.org

para Abuelita Neli
y sus hijas

. . .los que nunca sabe nadie de dónde son. . . los que fueron cosidos a balazos al cruzar la frontera. . . los eternos indocumentados. . .

. . .the ones no one ever knows where they're from. . . the ones burned by bullets when they crossed the border. . . the eternally undocumented. . .

Roque Dalton, "Poema de amor"
May 14, 1935–May 10, 1975

Contents

3 To Abuelita Neli

✝

7 Saguaros
8 *from* The Book I Made with a Counselor My First Week of School
9 Second Attempt Crossing
11 El Salvador
12 On a Dirt Road outside Oaxaca
13 Cassette Tape
15 To President-Elect
16 Pump Water from the Well
17 Instructions for My Funeral
18 Montage with Mangoes, Volcano, and Flooded Streets

✝

21 The Pier of La Herradura
23 Dancing in Buses
24 How to Enlist
25 Documentary
26 ARENA
27 "Don Chepe"
28 Disappeared
29 Rooftop
30 This Was the Field
31 Politics
32 Aftermath
34 For Israel and María de los Ángeles

✜

41 Crybaby

42 Abuelita Neli's Garden with Parakeets Named Chepito

43 I Don't Want to Speak of "Don Chepe"

44 How I Learned to Walk

45 Postpartum

46 "Ponele Queso Bicho" Means Put Cheese on It Kid

48 Then, It Was So

50 Mom Responds to Her Shaming

51 Alterations

54 Aubade

56 Prayer

58 Abuelita Says Goodbye

✜

61 Let Me Try Again

63 Citizenship

65 San Francisco Bay and "Mt. Tam"

66 Doctor's Office First Week in This Country

69 Vows

70 Nocturne

72 Deportation Letter

74 Seeing Your Mother Again

75 Exiliados

✜

79 June 10, 1999

92 Acknowledgments

94 About the Author

Unaccompanied

To Abuelita Neli

This is my 14th time pressing roses in fake passports
for each year I haven't climbed marañón trees. I'm sorry
I've lied about where I was born. Today, this country
chose its first black president. Maybe he changes things.
I've told Mom I don't want to have to *choose* to get married.
You understand. Abuelita, I can't go back *and* return.
There's no path to papers. I've got nothing left but dreams
where I'm: the parakeet nest on the flor de fuego,
the paper boats we made when streets flooded,
or toys I buried by the foxtail ferns. ¿Do you know
the ferns I mean? The ones we planted the first birthday
without my parents. I'll never be a citizen. I'll never
scrub clothes with pumice stones over the big cement tub
under the almond trees. Last time you called, you said
my old friends think that now I'm from some town
between this bay and our estero. And that I'm a coconut:
brown on the outside, white inside. Abuelita, please
forgive me, but tell them they don't know shit.

✠ ✠ ✠

Saguaros

It was dusk for kilometers and bats in the lavender sky,
    like spiders when a fly is caught, began to appear.
And there, not the promised land but barbwire and barbwire

    with nothing growing under it. I tried to fly that dusk
after a bat said *la sangre del saguaro nos seduce.* Sometimes
    I wake and my throat is dry, so I drive to botanical gardens

to search for red fruits at the top of saguaros, the ones
    at dusk I threw rocks at for the sake of hunger.

But I never find them here. These bats *speak English only.*
    Sometimes in my car, that viscous red syrup
clings to my throat and I have to pull over—

    I also scraped needles first, then carved
those tall torsos for water, then spotlights drove me
    and thirty others dashing into paloverdes;

green-striped trucks surrounded us and our empty bottles
    rattled. When the trucks left, a cold cell swallowed us.

from **The Book I Made with a Counselor**
   My First Week of School

His grandma made the best pupusas, the counselor wrote next to
      Stick-Figure Abuelita
                      (I'd colored her puffy hair black with a pen).

Earlier, Dad in his truck: "always look gringos in the eyes."
          Mom: "never tell them everything, but smile, always smile."

A handful of times I've opened the book to see running past cacti
             from helicopters, running inside detention cells.

Next to what might be yucca plants or a dried creek:
         Javier saw a dead coyote animal, which stank and had flies over it.

I keep this book in an old shoebox underneath the bed. She asked in Spanish,
         I just smiled, didn't tell her, *no animal, I knew that man.*

Second Attempt Crossing

for Chino

In the middle of that desert that didn't look like sand
    and sand only,
in the middle of those acacias, whiptails, and coyotes, someone yelled
    "¡La Migra!" and everyone ran.
In that dried creek where forty of us slept, we turned to each other,
    and you flew from my side in the dirt.

Black-throated sparrows and dawn
    hitting the tops of mesquites.
Against the herd of legs,

    you sprinted back toward me,
I jumped on your shoulders,
    and we ran from the white trucks, then their guns.

I said, "freeze Chino, ¡pará por favor!"

    So I wouldn't touch their legs that kicked you,
you pushed me under your chest,
    and I've never thanked you.

Beautiful *Chino*—

    the only name I know to call you by—
farewell your tattooed chest: the M,
    the S, the 13. Farewell
the phone number you gave me
    when you went east to Virginia,

and I went west to San Francisco.

You called twice a month,
then your cousin said the gang you ran from
    in San Salvador
found you in Alexandria. Farewell
    your brown arms that shielded me then,
that shield me now, from La Migra.

El Salvador

Salvador, if I return on a summer day, so humid my thumb
    will clean your beard of salt, and if I touch your volcanic face,

kiss your pumice breath, please don't let cops say: *he's gangster.*
    Don't let gangsters say: *he's wrong barrio.* Your barrios

stain you with pollen. Every day cops and gangsters pick at you
    with their metallic beaks, and presidents, guilty.

Dad swears he'll never return, Mom wants to see her mom,
    and in the news: black bags, more and more of us leave.

Parents say: *don't go; you have tattoos. It's the law; you don't know
    what law means there.* ¿But what do they know? We don't

have greencards. Grandparents say: *nothing happens here.*
    Cousin says: *here, it's worse. Don't come, you could be. . .*

Stupid Salvador, you see our black bags, our empty homes,
    our fear to say: *the war has never stopped,* and still you lie

and say: *I'm fine, I'm fine,* but if I don't brush Abuelita's hair,
    wash her pots and pans, I cry. Tonight, how I wish

you made it easier to love you, Salvador. Make it easier
    to never have to risk our lives.

On a Dirt Road outside Oaxaca

The Mexican never said how long.
¿How long? *Not long.* ¿How much?
Not much. Never told us we'd hide in vans like matchsticks.

In our town, we'd never known Mexicans
besides the women and men in soap operas,

so in our heads, we played the fence,
the San Ysidro McDonald's, a quick run, a van.

Not long, not long at all. In Oaxaca,
a small brown lizard licks horchata from my hand—
we're friends, we pick names for each other.

Hola Paula. *Hola Javier,* she says.
We play the fence, a quick run, the van. . .

¿How long? *Not long.* On the dirt,
our knees tell truths to the cops' front-sights and barrels.
¿How much? *Not much.*

We'd never known Mexicans besides Chente,
Chavela Vargas. We're on the dirt
like dogs showing nipples

to offspring, it's not spring,
and we're going to where there is spring,

we say *it's gonna be alright,*
it's gonna be just fine—
my hands play with Paula.

Cassette Tape

A

To cross México we're packed in boats
twenty aboard, eighteen hours straight to Oaxaca.
Vomit and gasoline keep us up. At 5 a.m.
we get to shore, we run to the trucks, cops
rob us down the road—without handcuffs,
our guide gets in their Ford and we know
it's all been planned. Not one peso left
so we get desperate—*Diosito, forgive us*
for hiding in trailers. We sleep in Nogales till
our third try when finally I meet Papá Javi.

》

Mamá, you left me.   Papá, you left me.
Abuelos, I left you.   Tías, I left you.
Cousins, I'm here.   Cousins, I left you.
Tías, ~~welcome.~~   Abuelos, we'll be back soon.
Mamá, let's return.   Papá ¿por qué?
Mamá, marry for papers.   Papá, marry for papers.
Tías, abuelos, cousins, be careful.
I won't marry for papers.   ~~I might marry for papers.~~
I won't be back soon.   I can't vote anywhere,
I will etch visas on toilet paper and throw them from a lighthouse.

《

When I saw the coyote—
I didn't want to go
but parents had already paid.
I want to pour their sweat,
each step they took,
and braid a rope.

I want that cord
to swing us back to our terracota roof.
No, I wanted to sleep
in my parents' apartment.

        B

You don't need more than food,
a roof, and clothes on your back.
I'd add Mom's warmth, the need
for war to stop. Too many dead
cops, too many tattooed dead.
¿Does my country need more of us
to flee with nothing but a bag?
Corrupt cops shoot "gangsters"
from armored cars. *Javiercito,*
parents say, *we'll send for you soon.*

        »

Last night, Mom wanted to listen to "Lulu's Mother,"
        a song she plays for the baby she babysits.

I don't know why this song gets to me, she said, then:

"Ahhhh Lu-lu-lu-lu / don't you cry / Mom-ma won't go / a-way /
Ahhhh Lu-lu-lu-lu / don't you cry / Pop-pa won't go / a-way. . ."

It's mostly other nannies in the class; *it's supposed to help*
        with the babies' speech development, she says, *mijo,*

sorry for leaving. I wish I could've taken you to music classes.

She reached over, crying. *Mom, you can sing to me now,*
        was all I could say, *you can sing to me now.*

To President-Elect

There's no fence, there's a tunnel, there's a hole in the wall, yes,
you think right now ¿no one's running? Then who is it that sweats
and shits their shit there for the cactus. We craved water; our piss
turned the brightest yellow—I am not the only nine-year-old
who has slipped my backpack under the ranchers' fences. I'm still
in that van that picked us up from "Devil's Highway." The white van
honked three times, honks heard by German shepherds, helicopters,
Migra trucks. I don't know where the drybacks are who ran with dogs
chasing after them. Correction: I do know. At night, they return
to say *sobreviviste bicho, sobreviviste carnal*. Yes, we over-lived.

Pump Water from the Well

This is no shatter and stone.

    Come skip toes in my chest, Salvador.

I'm done been the shortest shore.

    ¿And did you love all the self out of you for me?

I want you to torch the thatch above my head.

    To be estero. To be mangroves.

There are mornings I wake with taste of tortillas in warmed-up milk.

    There are pomegranates no one listens to.

¿Is this the mierda you imagined for me?

    Everywhere is war.

The patch of dirt I pumped water from to bathe.

    Chickens, dogs, parakeets, this was my block.

The one I want to shut off with rain.

    Where I want to plant an island.

Barrio Guadalupe hijueputa born and bred cerote ¿qué onda?

    The most beautiful part of my barrio was stillness

and a rustling of wings caught in the soil calling me to repair it.

    Don't tell me I didn't bring the estero up north where there's none.

I've walked uptown. I saw Mrs. Gringa.

    The riff between my fingers went down in whirlpools.

Silence stills me. Pensé quedarme aquí I said.

    I don't understand she said. From my forehead,

the jaw of a burro, hit on the side and scraped by a lighter to wake the song

    that speaks two worlds.

The kind of terrifying current.

    The kind of ruinous wind.

Instructions for My Funeral

Don't burn me in no steel furnace, burn me
        in Abuelita's garden. Wrap me in blue-
white-and-blue [a la mierda patriotismo].
        Douse me in the cheapest gin. Whatever you do,
don't judge my home. Cut my bones
        with a machete till I'm finest dust
[wrap my pito in panties so I dream of pisar].
        Please, no priests, no crosses, no flowers.
Steal a flask and stash me inside. Blast music,
        dress to impress. Please be drunk
[miss work y pisen otra vez].
        Bust out the drums the army strums.
Bust out the guitars guerrilleros strummed
        and listen to the war inside [please
no american mierdas]. Carouse the procession
        dancing to the pier. Moor me
in a motorboat [de veras que sea una lancha]
        driven by a nine-year-old
son of a fisherman. Scud to the center
        of the Estero de Jaltepec. Read
"Como tú," and toss pieces of bread.
        As the motorboat circles,
open the flask, so I'm breathed like a jacaranda,
        like a flor de mayo,
like an alcatraz—then, forget me
        and let me drift.

Montage with Mangoes, Volcano, and Flooded Streets

I helped Abuelita pluck the white flor de izote from stems
        to put in the bowl to then drop in the pan
                to mix with eggs,

there's no way Mom, younger than I am now
        and in California like I am now,
                there's no way she knew my technique:

grab stalk and pull toward belly,
        bowl between legs, petals like rice
                from opened burlap.

I'm older than Dad then,
        for the longest time I wanted to throw rocks
                at fruit bats, wanted to run

out of the kitchen to climb the big mango tree,
        branch by branch, up six meters
                to watch the volcano's peak fit in my hand—

lie to me. Say I can go back.
        Say I've created smoke and no rain.
                It's almost twenty years and still

I can't keep mangoes from falling six meters down,
        to where dogs lick what my aunts,
                Mom, Dad, and I still cannot.

✝ ✝ ✝

The Pier of La Herradura

When I sleep I see a child
    hidden between the legs of a scarred man:

their sunburned backs sweat cold air,
    the child faces me

and the pier's thatched roof swallows the moon
    cut by the clouds behind them.

Sometimes, they're on the same roof
    wearing handkerchiefs

and uniformed men surround them.
    I mistake bullet casings

for cormorant beaks diving
    till water churns the color of sunsets,

stained barnacles line the pier
    and I can't see who's facedown

on the boats painted crimson.
    Once, I heard the man—

alive and still on the roof—say
    today for you, tomorrow for me.

There's a village where men train cormorants
    to fish: rope-end tied to sterns,

another to necks, so their beaks
    won't swallow the fish they catch.

My father is one of those birds.
    He's the scarred man.

Dancing in Buses

Pretend a boom box
blasts over your shoulder. Raise
your hands in the air. Twist them
as if picking limes. Look
to the right as if crossing
streets. Look to the left,
slowly as if balancing orange
baskets. Bend as if picking
cotton. Do the rump. Straighten
up as if dropping firewood. Rake,
do the rake. Sweep,
do the sweep. Do the Pupusa-
Clap—finger dough clumps. Clap.
Do the Horchata-Scoop—
your hand's a ladle, scoop.
Reach and scoop. Now,
duck. They're shooting. Duck
under the seat, and
don't breathe.

Hands behind your head.
Drop down.
Look at the ground.
Roll over.
Face the mouth of the barrel.
Do the protect-face-with-hand.
Don't scream.

How to Enlist

for María de los Ángeles

You must meet in the bleachers during a packed fútbol game. She'll slip a paper with the assignment *meet by the dried creek*. Try to memorize her face. At midnight, she'll bring her thoughts wrapped in tamales and tell you to taste each one. That you didn't notice drunks unconscious on streets like kilometer markers won't matter. You'll train in warehouses for months till at the other end of overgrown cane fields, hidden by cashew groves, someone cleaning barrel, bolt, and chamber will greet you. Her laughter will fill you. Laughter saying: *The Final Offensive.* Shoes like banana peels in a landfill; these will be her shoes. *We can't use him,* she'll say and take shoelace, hands, belts, shirts, till her thoughts turn into dark spots in a ditch where fumes lick her skin. Don't forget her voice. Vow to avenge her name.

Documentary

from *The Houses Are Full of Smoke* (1987)

"One day, my mom came running
said ¿How can it be, the dogs
in the fútbol field?

So she asked for money
to buy a casket. I didn't know why,
she'd seen so many like that.

Neighbors tell me last night
they took so-and-so
found them in such-and-such place,

¿Who took them? ¿Who?
¿Ay por qué? I say.

We're scared, it's getting closer,
patrols grease their faces.

Then, someone came running.
They'd found her at El Playón,

she was wearing shorts. Dogs.
So many dogs. My mother
never wore shorts."

ARENA

Ay mamita, ¿don't you know Alianza Republicana Nacionalista's acronym spells sand? Don Vaquero's blue pickup truck drives by every hour. Those loudspeakers tell us this is the tide that will wash everything. Ay mamita, this is the party of Roberto D'Aubuisson who splits watermelons with machetes to show "everyone is red inside." People say D'Aubuisson is a close friend of un tal Tío Reagan and that his wife has a culo like Miss Universo.

ARENA's cheerleaders wear red-white-and-blue dresses; they're the girls older guys whistle at. At least, these are days boys get free plastic balls and we get free plastic pom-poms. There's Don Vaquero's pickup again. Last week he delivered the white voting booths. Behind those black curtains, my father dyed his thumb purple. Ay mamita, I shouldn't have told him I thought his print looked like the beach, the one with all those washed-up bullet casings.

—Mom, age 13

"Don Chepe"

The war is or isn't over, but coffee still brews,
sugar keeps vanishing, he's burned his uniform
and never wears boots, his daughters
break mirrors on him to save their mother
when he returns waking neighbors,
waking his grandson. His hammock is wet,
so are his pants, the parakeet,
a windup clock, his daughters in nightgowns,
his grandson in their arms,
his black boots don't make towns flee anymore—

Don has always been the wrong word:
redacted addresses, .38s, clips in back-pockets.
To see how many he'll kill, his grandson
throws rocks at tadpoles. One by one
his daughters leave. *Don* has always been
what his wife didn't know how to wash
from uniforms. His grandson's asked
to fetch vodka when *Don* tries to forget
the still-opened eyes. Not even that wakes him.
No one can cover mirrors in time.
No one can find the scorpion in their shoes.

Disappeared

Hold these names responsible: *ARENA, Roberto D'Aubuisson, Escuadro-*
nes de la Muerte, Las Fuerzas Armadas, Batallón Atlacatl, La Guardia
Civil, Escuela de las Américas (also known as: Fort Benning or Western
Hemisphere Institute for Security Cooperation), Batallón Atonal, Bush Sr.,
Ronald Reagan, Batallón Ramón Belloso, Alliance for Progress, USAID,
Batallón Eusebio Bracamonte, CIA, Jimmy Carter, Batallón Manuel José
Arce, the fourteen families. . .

Rooftop

for Tía Mali

On top of those tiles,
they thought they saw stars fall
as they imagined snow would
from an orange tree.

They saw them burst
bright yellow, bright
green, sometimes
red, on the ground,
on the roofs,
on the streets, a few
kilometers away,
in the islands,
in the cane.

They climbed the roof
when they heard boots
flash-flood through houses,
and when they felt the ground shiver,
they did not tremble.

She held her two-year-old
nephew, saying
Javiercito, they will stop falling
soon. It's just snow.

This Was the Field

Some say it's true—I haven't seen it—not here close to the coast. Doña Raquel says the islands are where bombs come from. She says those people are guerrilleros, their dogs carry messages, and their children are born with sickles up their asses. Teniente Milton says guerrilleros are scared of this town. Last week, Milton broke four of Carlito's fingers. If it weren't for Carlito's mother swearing she would beat the shit out of him—I don't know—Milton dragged him to the middle of the street and pointed the M16 at his forehead. That Las Fuerzas will shoot kids for listening to the radio—I don't know—I haven't seen it here. It started early one morning—the helicopter flying low to the ground—this happened five days in a row—one shipment an hour. Mamá Socorro says guerrilleros might be winning. It was the first time a helicopter flew over our town. All we read and heard about were battles in Tecoluca, the islands, the capital, the volcanoes. I ran under the helicopter, it never landed—it just threw bodies onto the field.

—Dad, age 11

Politics

If you shoot hummingbirds and eat their hearts,
you can shoot anything,

their father told them
walking them to and from that forest

where for twelve years
hummingbirds fought for hibiscus.

Look, this is how I did it,
the oldest says, arms outstretched,

imagining crosshairs in his old scope.
A good sniper, an obedient son.

The young one, my father,
the student who hid

a red handkerchief in his drawer,
looks at his hands, same width,

same color as his brother's
who repeats, *I had to. I had to.*

Aftermath

Condoms trapped in mangroves, sometimes
    shrapnel, and always that rotted scent
of abandoned pelican nests. Graffiti
    and old campaign posters taped
to the pier's stores where tourists once bought
    cocktails from yachts. But that's

neither here nor there, now there's foreign films
    played at the old baker's house
with the only TV, people out the door,
    no one translating. See,
little has changed. Burned thatch-roof,
    you can still stop rain. Bullet holes

in doors, we can see through you.
    Little has changed. Uniforms
aren't soldiers or guerrilleros—
    they're tattoos or policemen.
Storks and pelicans have been spotted
    deep in the estero like before

the bombs and there's talk crocodiles
    are back; still, some people
won't come, appear, they'll never be
    welcomed. See, little has changed.
Clay pots blacken and blacken. Little
    frog in the puddle, quiet now,

that's a beautiful song, but let us sleep
    a few more minutes now

between the lull of a fight between
    two gangs. Little frog, she'll come
if she wants, she's heard, frog,
    she's heard you.

For Israel and María de los Ángeles

I.

My uncle, Israel, and his fiancée, María, were among the first victims of the war in my hometown. Renato Quintanilla, the high-school teacher's brother, force-injected my uncle with a mixture of unidentified drugs. A few days later, María was raped and murdered by three soldiers under the command of Sargento Cachaca. My mother, then nine years old, found María in the public latrines. Israel became one of the town's locos before, a few months later, he completely disappeared. Mi familia still does not know where he is.

II.

I wasn't born when all this happened. I've learned to lower my eyelids
So blood looks like dirt. In dreams—a desire to see my uncle

Float from my kitchen past the chicken coop where there's shade.
The space modules he threw from trees say *if he'd been an astronaut,*

He would've been Israel *Armstrong.* I can't remember his voice. When I wake,
My toes pinch and my shirt shortens and the moon says *this is a sign.*

For the longest time, my father believed Israel was rained on by bombs,
Shadow in rivers, ditch in the dark. Precisely, radio reporters started
      countdowns

Backward. But from my uncle's nose, we think, shrapnel never burst.
My father still carries unopened water bottles in case he finds him.

III.

He wasn't a Zamora: a loudmouth, a drunk, a dumbfuck,
A thief, or a good-for-nothing, like the rest of us.

He was first to finish dictionaries, first to approach gringos
And speak "inglish." By then, La Herradura already sang his name.

He looked like Bruce Lee, taught himself kung fu and nunchaku
From mail-order catalogues. When he spoke, teachers took notes.

Every evening, he was last to leave the library. This was when
He learned to steal flowers for a woman other than his mother.

María loved his smile, the way he wrote her lines like
Mi Carita de Ángel, aquí tenés las flores más lindas.

IV.

Curfews, María walked toward him whispering
When the owl hoots three times, amor, that's death.

May this be yesterday when he choked with her voice,
Not the day his first word was *nada.*

Her breath, that sweet mango scent, her body, whitened from bedsheets
Tightened around her neck, her hair, coiled nets dragged ashore—

They pinned her limbs to dirt. No ropes. People said
She was a guerrillera, that she was the one

Who came back to this town, that Israel did steal,
That she did tie red scarves at La Nacional,

That he was the first to disarm guards.
Flies buzz in a jar.

V.

Years later, like those men,
I would tie wrists

To a bedframe
Till my teeth would lick

This and walk out of my
Lover's room.

VI.

Some say you still pace some street without the chain around your foot
That kept you home. You went crazy. Only the streets know.

We're tired of looking at strangers' left feet
To see if the big toe and the two next to that are missing.

Uncle, your brothers gave your mother the key
To the steel chain tied to your right foot,

The good one. Around her neck, the key waits for you.
This was after Las Fuerzas splintered María's door,

After her mother was a thud silenced by rifles, after the four times
You convinced enough patients to make a ladder

For you to break out of the psych ward, after
Your brothers tied you to the mangrove trunk,

After you escaped to visit María's cross
And after you got into a blue pickup truck.

Word was you'd been the last to see the saucepan in the sky.
Word was you beat the shit out of soldiers again,

Those hijueputas, who lit a firecracker in your foot,
At gunpoint of course—

    VII.

Uncle, I swing on the hammock you slept in;
I've never heard so many roosters. After you left

We weren't allowed to speak of María. On the 30th year
From the day she died, in another country—

There was salt on my father's cheeks and he said
Sand is his skin. ¿You know that right mijo? Uncle,

Our little "astro-nut" jumping off the pier
With your head in a fish-tank. What we do is stare

At the beach for you. We wait for spume
To touch our cheeks. This is what we do

Sometimes when we can't sleep. No.
This is what we don't do *some* times. In the water

We say the lines you wrote thirty years ago.
In case we find you.

‡ ‡ ‡

País mío no existes
sólo eres una mala silueta mía
una palabra que le creí al enemigo.

    Roque Dalton

Crybaby

All I was was a chillón.
Neighbors lined up against our fence
while the nurse checked for fever.
Mom called me her ear's fruit fly.
Even backyard mangoes said
¡Callá este chillón diosmío!

Abuelita says everyone brushed ash-toothpaste
with horsehair toothbrushes, that Mom
had a baker's sleep schedule,
that before 4 a.m., bakers once baked "bagels"
for tourists. My town hates bagels. I'm nine
and I've never seen a bagel.

I don't remember how tourists tipped.
Before I was born, the dawn locomotion of troops
was the town's alarm. Abuelita says
the aftertaste of ashes is moth wings,
arid powder where names are buried.

Those gringos wore uniforms
and threw coins into the tide
so boys reached for copper
from El Norte, where dusk is honey.
Abuelita says mangoes begged god,
¡Callá estos gringos diosmío!

I know no one slept before my birth.
For years after,
still, no one slept.

Abuelita Neli's Garden with Parakeets Named Chepito

Abuelita's mother died when she was one.
No one talks about Great-Great-Grandma
or how Abuelita draws her eyebrows on at dawn.
I saw them once
when I pretended to snore.

Abuelita's name should be Rocio
because she wakes at 5 to water plants,
her name means truth
in some language no one speaks.

Grandpa says Abuelita burned the beans
otra vez. Chepito the Fourth dreams of tortillas
when Grandpa swings in the hammock. Abuelita,
¿pero why you don't have eyebrows?

Sometimes Abuelita dries her bras on rosebushes.
Doña Avalos thinks she grows the best roses,
so when they walk to the market
their baskets bounce on opposite sides.

I forgot to feed Chepito the Third for a week.
I said the cat ate Chepito the Second
and when he became dough below my feet
I buried the first Chepito.

Grandpa cuts our parakeet's wings and dips our moons
in vodka. Truth is, before I drowned
Chepito the Fourth, I asked him if he remembered
the eggshell he broke. Abuelita, ¿will you forget
the veins on the back of Grandpa's hands?

I Don't Want to Speak of "Don Chepe"

He has chased all of us up the street to the market waving his machete. Of my two sisters, the eldest never returned, he caught her with a man not her husband and cut a dahlia on her dress. The youngest hid in the banana groves, she told him she was pregnant. We inherited our jawline from his father—murdered by another woman's husband at the cantina. Typical. When he's calm, he rakes mounds of leaves and trash, rolls and lights newspaper, watches flames almost choke the lowest almond branches. I know he thinks of his wife, his two sons, the ones before us, and why they left him. He speaks of them only when he, drunk, tells me to play Javier Solís records. If I split a leaf with my nail, I smell embers erase yesterday's headlines: *The Oro Bridge bombed by guerrillas.* Between the lit mounds, I see my sisters waiting to throw water, to hear ashes: curl, sizzle, smoke.

—Tía Mali, age 16

How I Learned to Walk

Callâte. Don't say it out loud: the color of his hair,
the sour odor of his skin, the way they say
his stomach rose when he slept. I have
done nothing, said nothing. I piss in the corner
of the room, the outhouse is far, I think
orange blossoms call me to eat them. I fling rocks
at bats hanging midway up almond trees.
I've skinned lizards. I've been bored. It's like
that time I told my friend Luz to rub her lice
against my hair. I wanted to wear a plastic bag,
to smell of gasoline, to shave my hair, to feel
something like his hands on my head.
When I clutch pillows, I think of him. If he sleeps
facedown like I do. If he can tie strings
to the backs of dragonflies. I've heard
of how I used to run to him. His hair still
smelling of fish, gasoline, and seaweed. It's how
I learned to walk, they say. Callâte. If I step
out this door, I want to know nothing will take me.
Not the van he ran to. Not the man he paid to take him.
Mom was asleep when he left. People say
somehow I walked across our cornfield
at dawn, a few steps behind. I must have seen him
get in that van. I was two. I sat behind a ceiba tree,
waiting. No one could find me.

Postpartum

My son's in the other room. This little
burlap sack of rice came out yellow,
some deficiency, got incubated, hasn't
stopped crying—his father wasn't there,
he was "out fishing." His father's mother came
next day saying, I'm saint I'm saint,
I won't let you trick him. "The big saint"
wanted to check my son for birthmarks
to see if he's really Zamora. She found them
near his balls. Esa puta didn't even give
enough for powdered milk. And don't
tell me he looks like his father, maybe
the back of his hair. I know his father
doesn't love me. You don't have to tell me:
you're stupid, you're jealous, crazy.
Maybe he hears, I wish he hears my moans
when he's on top of his whores.
Like I don't know. I am crazy, but not
estúpida. If I catch him, me las va pagar.
Me las va pagar, that dipshit
deep in debt over a fishing boat
he can't catch nothing in. My son
won't drink from me. I pump breasts,
rub sugar and honey on them,
¿why won't he drink from me?

—Mom, age 18

"Ponele Queso Bicho" Means Put Cheese on It Kid

for Miguel Alcántara, aka La Belleza

¿Why you post on my fence and wait for water, Belleza?

    ¿You don't know? I'm Rambo.
    Look at these muscles, they shine like desks.
    Va. Call me Sevestre Escalon.

It's pronounced Sil-vés-tre, Belleza. Sil-vés-tre Es-ta-lón.

    Comé mierda bicho. I made the best desks.
    I had a shop. Ponele queso,
    every night I cut where branch meets trunk.

¿When you gone make me a desk then?

    I made desks. Ponele queso.
    ¿You know what that means?
    When I die my phrase is gone be on TV,
    it'll be like Sevestre in that movie *Cobra*.
    He'll try to figure what that shit means.
    Puta bicho, I'll be famous.

It's Sil-vés-tre, Belleza. And yes, I know what it means.

    ¿What it mean then?

Sounds like those mazes with the cheese in the middle and a rat outside.

    Va. Va. Va. You do use that coconut.
    I knew you were your father.

¿You knew my father?

> Don't touch the tiger's balls.
> I made the smoothest desks. Ponele queso.
> It's all in the smell bicho.

¿Did my father say that?

> You're touching the balls. You're touching the balls.
> But look, it's something like when you go to the store
> and vodka is two colones ¿right?

Right.

> The label says 80 proof. But rubbing alcohol is one colón,
> 200 proof. So I wait for you to bring water.

¿What does that mean?

> Look, I was passed out when he got in that van.
> He had a backpack. You were asleep. He didn't want to go.
> But the dólares and war bicho. Ponele queso.
> Ponele queso and the rat won't leave.

Then, It Was So

To tell you I was leaving
I waited and waited
rethinking first sentences in my sleep,
I didn't sleep,
and my heart was a watermelon
split each night. Outside,
3 a.m. was the same as bats
and you were our kerosene lamp.

Amor, I thought it was something
we were in that day, hiding
from bullets in sugarcane, my chest
pressed against the gossamers
stuck to your thighs,
when stars swam inside you.

The last second has passed
and I can't forget one centimeter.
To kiss each cheek,
your lips, your forehead.
I miss our son. I miss the faint wick
on his skin. How I held him
and how I wanted to then, though
I didn't wake him.

That dawn, I needed to say
you remind me of my father
and leaving is a bucket of mosquitoes
no one empties. Cariño,

it was so quiet when I started
counting the days
I wasn't woken by him.

—Dad, age 19

Mom Responds to Her Shaming

Dad chased me out of the house again with his machete
¿what would you have done? You're up north,

I waited twenty-three months to date ¿and you say
you won't speak to *me*? You must know

I'm not allowed to see our son. That I sleep
in the street because "my boyfriends"

won't open their doors. No one will open.
Hijueputa, I was seventeen, the valedictorian,

you wouldn't use a condom. Give me back
the minutes you'd undress me under

the grapefruit tree. Your new girlfriend,
your sisters say she's a faithful one. Hipócrita,

I'm the one that caught you with La Salivosa,
no one believes me. I wish you knew

what it's like to hide from my dad
and wait for him to pass out so I can hold

my son's cheeks as I try to explain—
I can't stay here.

Alterations

She says she lit a candle and placed it under my balls when I was born
because they were too big,
of course you don't want that. Then

there's wetting your fingers with spit
to pull the nose in the morning so it's straight.

And it was straight
till I broke it turning the corner
playing tag in first grade.

You shat on your face, Mom said,
and hit me nowhere near my face.

She hit me when I broke my hand,
the branch of the sweetsop tree
too thin for me to hang from.

Two days it took
to take me to the hospital.

First she pulled me by the other arm,
hit my ass with a stick. Time-out,

she locked me in a room.
When she saw my arm swell,
she took me to the witch doctor
who spat tobacco
and rubbed me with ruda leaves
then blew smoke.

Heal heal little frog's butt,
he said, I thought it worked.

We were poor. We sold pupusas
to patients. In the next room
a kid was tied to his bed.

It's a thing that happens the real doctor said.
The Jell-O was my favorite part
of wearing a cast. But I liked it all,

the not showering, the plastic bag over it
when I had to shower
in front of the well in my underwear.

The birds. Mom with a towel.
Earthworms in the dirt. Wind.
Her fingers drying my hair. The flies
hovering over my arm.
The smell.

We never went back to the doctor
to cut the cast. Mom used a saw
once my arm didn't hurt
when I stuck a stick down it
when it itched.

She kept rubbing my arm
with red-fox oil first thing
in the morning,

passed a candle along my skin
dropped three drops of wax

then rubbed them toward my fingers
lightly, lightly,
the bones didn't crack.

Aubade

I'll be back soon mijo—

           but in our windows still no glass,
when raindrops hit the sill
           they touch my skin like her eyes did
that morning she said
                I'll be back soon mijo.
After the rains, too many mosquitoes
           so the clinic sent uniformed men
who sprayed a thick fog
               meant to kill larvae.
We covered bowls, pans, pots, and bottles,
            washed them by hand,
but Abuelita still
           "accidentally" broke my milk bottle
so I would stop asking for Mom.
               No glass in our windows.
I know she won't return,
           I've memorized the names of roads
I can't pronounce
           far from these volcanoes that know
what toys I don't let friends touch
           and in which drawer I keep the letters
Mom has sent me.
           I touch the larvae growing in old tires
in our backyard, I know
              she won't return.
Abuelita hid my letters
           with addresses I can't pronounce
so I would stop asking her

                              to read them to me
every night,
                         under this terracota roof,
under this candlelight.

Prayer

If nuns at school find out, guards
won't let me through. They did that
for Margarita. I can't tell anyone
I'm going to see my parents.
(¡I'm going to see my parents!)
If Mom was here, we'd split palm sticks
and I'd run to Doña Chita's,
buy shoemaker's glue, China paper,
nylon. Church bells just rang.
Diosito, guard my way across
the bean field, past Great-Great-Grandma's,
over the fútbol field, down the road
past Mom's best friend's. I gotta ask
Mother Superior how long
it takes to cross Guatemala, México.
Diosito, I've been eating broccoli,

drinking all my milk so parents
think I'm big. Mom and I would fly
long as it took the kite to crash. Often
it was the neighbor's avocado trees,
we'd pull and pull till the string broke,
neighbors would come and yell
but we weren't after their iguanas.
I don't like to eat iguanas like Mom.
I'm going to see my parents.
(¡I'm going to see my parents!)
On my last day of school, I'll tell
only my closest friends I'm flying
to where people drink cold milk,

put strawberries in their cereal,
I'll eat strawberries all the time
get so tall I'll start playing basketball.

Abuelita Says Goodbye

Javiercito, you're leaving me tomorrow
when our tortilla-and-milk breaths will whisper
te amo. When I'll pray the sun won't devour
your northbound steps. I'm giving you
this conch swallowed with this delta's
waves and the sound of absorbing sand.

Hold it to your ear. I'm tired
of my children leaving. My love for you
shatters windows with birds. Javiercito,
let your shadow return, alone,
or with sons, but soon. Call me Mamá,
not Abuelita. All my children

learned the names of seasons
from songs. Tonight, leaves fall.
There's no autumn here. When you mist
into tomorrow's dawns, at the shore
of somewhere, listen to this conch.
Don't lose me.

✚✚✚

Let Me Try Again

I could bore you with the sunset, the way water tasted
    after so many days without it,
                    the trees,
the breed of dogs, but I can't say
                    there were forty people
when we found the ranch with the thin white man,
        his dogs,
                and his shotgun.

Until this 5 a.m. I couldn't remember
                there were only five,
or seven people—

We'd separated by the paloverdes.
    We, meaning:
                four people. Not forty.
The rest. . .
    I don't know.
                They weren't there
when the thin white man
                let us drink from a hose
while pointing his shotgun.
                In pocho Spanish he told us
si correr perros atacar.
                If run dogs trained attack.

When La Migra arrived, an officer
    who probably called himself Hispanic at best,

not Mejicano like we called him, said
                buenas noches
    and gave us pan dulce y chocolate.

Procedure says he should've taken us
    back to the station,

checked our fingerprints,
                    etcétera.

He must've remembered his family
    over the border,

or the border coming over them,
    because he drove us to the border

and told us
    next time, rest at least five days,

don't trust anyone calling themselves coyotes,
    bring more tortillas, sardines, Alhambra.

He knew we would try again
    and again,
                    like everyone does.

Citizenship

it was clear they were hungry
with their carts empty the clothes inside their empty hands

they were hungry because their hands
were empty their hands in trashcans

the trashcans on the street
the asphalt street on the red dirt the dirt taxpayers pay for

up to that invisible line visible thick white paint
visible booths visible with the fence starting from the booths

booth road booth road booth road office building then the fence
fence fence fence

it started from a corner with an iron pole
always an iron pole at the beginning

those men those women could walk between booths
say hi to white or brown officers no problem

the problem I think were carts belts jackets
we didn't have any

or maybe not *the* problem
our skin sunburned all of us spoke Spanish

we didn't know how they had ended up that way
on *that* side

we didn't know how we had ended up here
we didn't know but we understood why they walk

the opposite direction to buy food on this side
this side we all know is hunger

San Francisco Bay and "Mt. Tam"

Every day there's the bay, every day, every night, once, it was Estero de Jaltepec:
    Kingdom of Sand: warm, coconut-sweet, not salt.
                                We jumped from the pier,
we jumped from mangroves when air was thick gold honey. We'd come up
    and there it was, El Volcán de Chinchontepec:
                              Mountain of Breasts:
dormant, with a cornfield-skirt. Twenty years above the tropic, every day,
    every night, there's "Mt. Tam," its Coast Miwok name
                              Tamalpais
shortened by gringos: foreign and invasive like pampas grass,
    like eucalyptus, like every single white seed of dandelions.

Doctor's Office First Week in This Country

it's procedure to inspect
the ass of an immigrant kid

undress put this gown on
the doctor will be here soon

that first day after Sonoran Desert
I showered for hours when we got to parents' apartment

Father showed me the way to turn the knob that first day
how things worked

I hadn't seen him since I was one
I didn't *know him* know him

this is how you make your pee-pee grow he said so it's bigger so it's
      the biggest
he said sometime that first month or that first year
pull
pull I did
pull
do it now
you're young
it will work he said

did anything happen the doctor asked in front of my parents
then alone
did anything happen along the way in Spanish
all of this in Spanish
starting with *es procedimiento*

this is how you get hot water
twist then pull

no
I'd never used a sponge
soap-bar and hand was enough back there next to a well

I'd never seen a "shower"
parents said it that way in English *chá-uer*

that first "shower"
my dirt drew a dark rim around the linoleum

you will hear from us next week
I came back for all the necessary shots

I grew up across the street from a clinic
every kid cried

I came back I got shot I didn't cry

I kept turning the wrong knob
even after Dad showed me

then Mom showed me
then we showered together

to make me comfortable with my own body again
with theirs
with anyone's

it burned that first time
my skin
hot water
nothing happened

it burned
I'm sure
seguro que
nada pasó

Vows

Ever since a brown girl wanted fifteen thousand from me
to marry her, I've vowed to not sign documents
to get a visa, then ask myself why
I've let that hurt me so much to never buy rings.

Amor, tell me to shut up, tell me none of that matters,
come watch the tide drain south
to where the house I left is lined with glass and barbwire.

When I call abuelos,
¡Ay no mijo! Someone else is dead. Then,
they ask about you. I'm four years older than them
when they got married, six years older
than my parents, always they ask when I'll visit,

soon Abuelos, soon. What I mean is
I can never go back. Amor, know more than I love you
quite possibly I love that bay at low tide,
even possibly, mangrove roots with bright-orange crabs.

You can't know what it's like to have that place
disappear, those brown waves, those bright-orange crabs,
what I really mean when I say *I can never go back*

is I wish to lie next to you every morning,
where we dive headfirst to know
what it's like to swim in the middle of love
and see each gull flee like clothes
bouncing off the wall to the carpet
we must pick clean like a beach, after hurricanes.

Nocturne

Tomorrow won't be the same, each step
farther from the border. Gin and tonics.
Tequila grapefruits. I threw that black mug
at your face after gin, after tequila,
I'm sorry. I drank too much. I drink too much,
I know. It wasn't me who threw it,
I said, but it was. I was four. I saw Mom
between Grandpa's gun and Grandma.
I was four. He chased every single
one of his daughters with his machete
in the middle of the day, in the middle of the night,
I didn't know what to do except climb
the water tower across the street
with Red Power Ranger. He's chased us
to this country that trained him to stay quiet
when "his boss" put prisoners in black bags,
then pushed them from the truck, "for everyone to see
what happens to bad people here." Gin,
straight up. Tequila shots. No one understands why
Abuelita never left him. It's mid-June,
Venus and Mars the closest they've been
in 2,000 years, but I've never seen grandparents hug,
or hold hands. I make an excuse.
You kept rubbing your hands. When I turned six
Grandpa quit drinking. He stayed at home at night
but never talked to us. He didn't like gin.
Didn't like writers. Didn't like leftists.
Everyone gone except one cousin. You're not here.
Tomorrow, tan poco. These walls snore
like Grandpa's slurred shouts. I thought
the border would take him. All my aunts,

my mom, thought so too. We're all running
from the sun on his machete.
The moon on his gun.

Deportation Letter

for my cousin Julia Zetino

The words *Notice to Appear* flap like a monarch trapped in a puddle.
Translation: ten years in a cell cold enough to be named Hielera.
If not that, a plane with chains locked to her legs. My aunt swam across
the Río Bravo twice to see her second daughter born in Greenbrae.
¿Why can't my sister come here? asks the one who speaks English.
The monarch's beaten, but it won't listen. Since nothing's wasted,
it might get eaten, it will nourish ants already gathering.

✝

*It was a hill like this. I was tired. I couldn't keep running and fell. If it wasn't for
the women who went back to pick me up from the shore, I wouldn't be here.*

✝

Somewhere along here there's a bridge. A cactus-pear bridge, red
like: the dirtiest sunset, Gila monster hiding, leftover sardines in tin.
¿The hibiscus sprouting? ¿Bougainvillea? One daughter wakes
and sees them and the volcano, and fire flowers through her window.
She's never seen the bridge her mom isn't afraid of.

✝

My aunt, twenty-five years selling pupusas near that pier, ten and counting
cleaning houses, baking bread, anything in Larkspur. Most people
in La Herradura haven't seen their parents. Her daughter Julia, over there.
Here, her daughter Adriana takes the bus to school every day.

✝

*The first try we were already in that van and La Migra was chasing us. The driver
said he was going to stop, we should open the doors and run. There were a lot of trucks.
Sirens. Men through the speakers. I got to a bush and hid. One dog found me.
He didn't bite. He just stood next to me till one gringo handcuffed me.*

✝

*This beach, these hills, are pretty. It looks like La Puntilla, except it's cold.
I wish Julia was here. Javier, take a picture of Adriana and me. I'll send it to Julia.*

✝

It's complicated. *Mamá me dejaste, decí que vas a regresar,* I said, at night
on that same bed you sleep in now. Same bed next to the window
from which you see the lemons, the custard apples, the bean fields,
then the volcano. I'm sorry none of us ever saw you draw butterflies
like we see Adriana draw them, with the caption: "the butterflies
were going to save the world from tornado. And did."

Seeing Your Mother Again

If you could cup your ears against all I've said:
    ants inside me, a disturbed mound. Mamá Pati,

those years you weren't there I throw at fronds,
    so I drink what I've been wanting. Your 24th birthday

I bought you a coconut and carved your name
    because "women become cracked," but no,

eventually they lick us, we open our eyes, drag ourselves
    out of our shoeboxes. Tails down. Forgiveness

is a lizard squirming. Mamá Pati, feed it to me.
    From your salt on my cheeks, I know

you read all my letters, machetes cutting husk.

Exiliados

for Monica Sok

We didn't hold typhoons or tropics in our hands.
    I didn't reach across the table on our first date
        at Cornelia Street Café. In my humid pockets,

my fists were old tennis balls thrown to the stray dog
    of love bouncing toward the Hudson down
        to South Ferry. We didn't hold hands in that cold

October wind, but the waves witnessed our promise
    to return to my cratered-deforested homeland,
        and you to your parents', sometime in the future.

Then, us in the subway at 2 a.m. Oh the things I dreamed:
    a kiss to the back of your neck, collarbone, belly button, there—
        to kneel and bow my head, then return to the mole

next to your lips and taste your latitude together.
    Instead, I went home, you touched my cheek,
        it was enough. I stood, remembering what it's like

to stand on desert dirt wishing stars would fall
    as rain, on that huge dark country ahead of me.

✝✝✝

My country you don't exist
you're only a bad silhouette of mine
a word I believed from the enemy.

Roque Dalton

June 10, 1999

I.

first day inside a plane I sat by the window
like when I ride the bus
correction when I rode buses
below the border I sat by the window attention
to dogs under a mango
trash under parked cars
drunks passed out

I sat by plane window
same afternoon I crossed
desert the third time
was not nervous at white
people at terminal all those questions
did not cry did not stop
looking out the window
for Statue of Liberty Golden
Gate Disneyland Miami

I.

we were lost and didn't know which star
was north what was east west we all
dropped out of the van too soon to remember
someone said the sun rose east we circled
so much we had no maps and the guide we paid
twisted his ankle was slowing us down

we couldn't leave him *why*
asked the ones who walked ahead
whispered they'd heard coyotes fake they're hurt
circle and circle so much they make it seem they tried
but all they did was steal money

I don't know
his ankle *was* swollen he *was* feverish
it's true
the sun's heat *was* a reptile but I know
if we hadn't left him we'd still be
run-over toads

I.

I didn't recognize Dad
different from pictures

he remembers the smell
shit piss dust in your hair
he says now
crying

Mom had a bag with Nikes
Levi's *Star Wars*
Episode One shirt

I left my ripped clothes
inside a Ross fitting room

I'm tired of writing *the fence   the desert*
the van picked us up
took me to parents
I'm tired it's always that

even now outside United Airlines 18F
I see clouds first like quilt
then like cheese
melting in a plastic bag
under *creosotes*
next to those *empty*
gallons of water

I.

Mom didn't know
Dad didn't know
even if they'd run across fences before
they didn't see my knees
crashing into cactus needles
that night one shoe slipped off

she says Coyote said
I'll carry him to your front door myself Pati

she didn't know 110 degrees
when like Colorado River toads
we slid under bushes

officers yelled
on your fucking knees

you couldn't have known this could happen
Mom
you couldn't have
no es su culpa
no lo es

I.

javier here you go
about same shit
when will your status change

when will you stop
not being that June 10
let it go man

you're not inside that Tucson fitting room
this is not Abuelita
who you couldn't call
those eight weeks she lit a candle every night
to light your path

Abuelita who you can't call
every two weeks
you can't even tell her la quiero
la quiero mucho
only here in a language
she don't speak

I.

I left Grandpa in Guatemala
for eight weeks no one heard my voice
for eight weeks
no one slept

twice parents packed the car said
I'm going to the border

then at 1 a.m.
someone called said
you the parent of javier nine years old
from El Salvador
yes

órale
it's gone be fifteen hundred
cash
can you get to Tucson
tomorrow
yes

órale
near Phoenix
call this number

I.

to write I look for words in books
little ants Abuelita calls words

right now it's *bonsai*
that makes me think *father*

he made the one in a black pot in the first living-room I saw
in this country

correction first *furnished* living-room in this country
my first dawn here I spent it dreaming
about what furniture should be where
on that living-room carpet used as coyote warehouse
in some Tucson suburb

the smell of all fifty of us who waited for family
to pay so we could take different vans
to different states

in that ceiling's white bumpy surface
I imagined a movie I wanted to see
Mi Vida Gringa

I was ready to be gringo
speak English
own a pool
Jeep convertible

I.

Abuelita won't leave the house
hasn't left in years
hasn't will not
leave
no bullshit
no metaphor

she won't shower
won't walk to the market
pero they'll talk
what will they say
she says

who is they
and who cares
we say through the phone
on the table
by her door
we've all walked out of

her hair knots a dread
in the back of her short hair

like a microphone head
cousin says

my little microphone head
won't shower
won't sit on a chair
watching people walk by
like she did
when we were there

I.

I wasn't born here
I've always known this country wanted me dead

do you believe me when I say more than once
a white man wanted me dead

a white man passed a bill that wants me deported
wants my family deported

a white man a white man a white man
not the song I wanted to hear

driving to the airport today
the road the trees the signs the sky the cars the walls the lights

told me   we want you
out out out out

I.

a few hours ago I boarded a plane
tried to cut ahead with Group A
usually I'm not caught I was stopped
the flight attendant told me wait
it's not your turn I started sweating
I wore white the worst
color for sweat my back drenched
until she let me through I was
in the gate in the plane 18F

when I got to SFO
I took Marin Airporter to San Rafael
same bus I took when I first saw
the Golden Gate
I'd never dreamed of it then
waiting in that line at the US embassy
when I tried and tried for a visa
like Mom like Dad like aunts
and we all got denied

I.

in public again writing at the corner
so people can't see line breaks
so they think I'm essayist

maybe I'm ashamed
maybe I don't want them reading this
that was not part of *Mi Vida Gringa*

Mi Vida Gringa not the movie I paid to see then
on that ceiling
but I still haven't exited in protest
haven't been kicked out
for not having a valid ticket
I sneaked in bought the popcorn drank the Coke
bonsai the word stuck in my brain
Dad a landscaper Mom a babysitter

I was supposed to be lawyer
businessman soccer player
Mom and Dad said
someone of value

I.

javier can you think of that date
without almost pissing yourself in La Migra's backseat
and in front of you people running
fast as we could

now I walk toward dawn
only when I'm fucked up
and if I'm blacked out
I want to shut the fuck up
those brown strangers
who didn't listen and ran
from Migra guns

but now in San Francisco
I'm half-drunk at 8 a.m.
stuffing shirts pants socks
into my carry-on
as if I had a flight today

I've carried this since that day
I'm talking about the flor de izote in our fence
the one Abuelita plucked
mixed with eggs that dawn she was crying
I didn't know why
come out come out of the house Abuelita
please

I'm soft I'm soft Grandpa says
who to this day goes out with his bad knee
to the fields and scrapes the grass
hunching down raking to blast the leaves on fire

and what do I do

I sit here type it's Monday
it's Tuesday it's Friday
type *first day inside a plane I sat by the window*

everyone's working
Mom Dad Tía Lupe Tía Mali
working under different names
I sit here writing our names

the TV is on
coffee is on
the couch is soft
my throat is dry
and sick and still
nothing has changed

Acknowledgments

Gracias Abuelita Neli por ser mi madre desde que nací, pero especial-
mente durante mis primeros nueve años. Abuelo, gracias por dejar de
tomar cuando mi mamá se fue.

Gracias Papá Javi por su apoyo, siempre. Mamá Pati, usted es un
gran ejemplo de una mujer fuerte y luchadora, gracias por todos sus
esfuerzos.

Tía Mali y Tía Lupe, gracias por ser mis hermanas mayores, por
cuidarme esos años, por las conversaciones.

Julia, que con este libro nos tengás más cerca, tan cerca como
quisiéramos estar de vos. Toñito y Adriana, que este libro les sirva a
entender algunas cosas.

Gracias familia, que sin su apoyo, sus esfuerzos, sus risas, sus historias,
pero principalmente, su amor, estas páginas no existieran. Los quiero
mucho y perdón si algunos días han llegado a dudar de mi amor.

Monica Sok, gracias mi Ocelota for coming into my life, for the walks,
the red string, your love.

To my CantoMundo and Macondo familia, sincere thank you for
holding space, for your tears, for your laughter, and warmth.

To Becky for helping me apply to Breadloaf, Napa Valley, Squaw
Valley, and VONA. Thank you to these workshops, where the seeds
for this book were first planted. Gracias Willie Perdomo for the
advice, the realness, and your work.

To Rigoberto Gonzalez and Eduardo Corral for your light that contin-
ues to provide that extra push I need, this book would not be possible
without you.

Thanks to Yusef Komunyakaa, Deborah Landau, Sharon Olds, and
Brenda Shaughnessy, who helped me with the early stages of this
manuscript. To Major Jackson and Marie Howe for your brilliance.
Thank you NYU.

To Louise Glück and Michael Wiegers for helping me in the final stages: your eyes were desperately needed, thank you.

To Peter Balakian, Casa Latina (Cristina, Denise, Anna), Chelsea, and everyone at Colgate who provided community in that coldest of winters, thank you.

To the Aninstantia Foundation, MacDowell Colony, the National Endowment for the Arts, the Poetry Foundation, Saltonstall Foundation, and Yaddo, for time and support.

Thank you to Eavan Boland and the cohort at the Wallace Stegner program for the workshops in which the last poems in this book were shaped.

A huge thank you to the editors of the publications in which some of these poems first appeared as is, or in earlier versions: *AGNI, American Poetry Review, Borderlands, Colorado Review, Crab Orchard Review, CONSEQUENCE Magazine, Day One, Diario Co Latino, elfaro, FENCE, Four Way Review, Gulf Coast, Granta, Huizache, Indiana Review, Kenyon Review, Meridian, NACLA, Narrative Magazine, New England Review, Ninth Letter, Notre Dame Review, PEN America Online, Ploughshares, Poetry Magazine, New Republic, New York Times, TriQuarterly, Virginia Quarterly Review, and Washington Square Review.*

Thank you to the following anthologies in which some of these poems appear:

> *Best New Poets 2013: 50 Poems from Emerging Writers*
> *Ghost Fishing: An Eco-Justice Poetry Anthology*
> *Misrepresented People: Poetic Responses to Trump's America*
> *The Wandering Song: Central American Writing in the United States*
> *Theatre under My Skin: Contemporary Salvadoran Poetry/Teatro bajo mi piel: poesía salvadoreña contemporanea*

Gracias all of you who've believed in me, who've shared memories, who've shared bread, un millón de gracias.

Finalmente, abrazos a todos los inmigrantes en todo el mundo, I believe in you.

About the Author

Javier Zamora was born in La Herradura, El Salvador, in 1990. He holds a BA from the University of California, Berkeley, where he studied and taught in June Jordan's Poetry for the People program. Zamora earned an MFA from New York University and is currently a 2016–2018 Wallace Stegner Fellow at Stanford University. He is the recipient of scholarships to the Bread Loaf, Frost Place, Napa Valley, Squaw Valley, and VONA writers' conferences and fellowships from CantoMundo, Colgate University (Olive B. O'Connor), MacDowell Colony, Macondo Foundation, National Endowment for the Arts, Saltonstall Foundation, and Yaddo. In 2016, Barnes & Noble granted him the Writer for Writers Award for his work with the Undocupoets Campaign. He was also the winner of the Ruth Lilly/Dorothy Sargent Fellowship and is a member of the Our Parents' Bones Campaign, whose goal is to bring justice to the families of the ten thousand disappeared during El Salvador's civil war. You can learn more about it www.ourparentsbones.org.

Lannan Literary Selections

For two decades Lannan Foundation has supported the publication and distribution of exceptional literary works. Copper Canyon Press gratefully acknowledges their support.

LANNAN LITERARY SELECTIONS 2017

John Freeman, *Maps*

Rachel McKibbens, *blud*

W.S. Merwin, *The Lice*

Javier Zamora, *Unaccompanied*

Ghassan Zaqtan (translated by Fady Joudah), *The Silence That Remains*

RECENT LANNAN LITERARY SELECTIONS FROM
COPPER CANYON PRESS

Josh Bell, *Alamo Theory*

Mark Bibbins, *They Don't Kill You Because They're Hungry, They Kill You Because They're Full*

Malachi Black, *Storm Toward Morning*

Marianne Boruch, *Cadaver, Speak*

Jericho Brown, *The New Testament*

Olena Kalytiak Davis, *The Poem She Didn't Write and Other Poems*

Michael Dickman, *Green Migraine*

Deborah Landau, *The Uses of the Body*

Sarah Lindsay, *Debt to the Bone-Eating Snotflower*

Maurice Manning, *One Man's Dark*

Camille Rankine, *Incorrect Merciful Impulses*

Roger Reeves, *King Me*

Paisley Rekdal, *Imaginary Vessels*

Brenda Shaughnessy, *So Much Synth*

Richard Siken, *War of the Foxes*

Frank Stanford, *What About This: Collected Poems of Frank Stanford*

Ocean Vuong, *Night Sky with Exit Wounds*

Poetry is vital to language and living. Since 1972, Copper Canyon Press has published extraordinary poetry from around the world to engage the imaginations and intellects of readers, writers, booksellers, librarians, teachers, students, and donors.

WE ARE GRATEFUL FOR THE MAJOR SUPPORT PROVIDED BY:

THE PAUL G. ALLEN
FAMILY FOUNDATION

Anonymous

Jill Baker and Jeffrey Bishop

Donna and Matt Bellew

John Branch

Diana Broze

Sarah and Tim Cavanaugh

Janet and Les Cox

Mimi Gardner Gates

Linda Gerrard and Walter Parsons

Gull Industries, Inc.
on behalf of Ruth and William True

The Trust of Warren A. Gummow

Steven Myron Holl

Phil Kovacevich and Eric Wechsler

Lakeside Industries, Inc.
on behalf of Jeanne Marie Lee

TO LEARN MORE ABOUT UNDERWRITING
COPPER CANYON PRESS TITLES,
PLEASE CALL 360-385-4925 EXT. 103

WE ARE GRATEFUL FOR THE MAJOR SUPPORT PROVIDED BY:

Lannan

ART WORKS.

National
Endowment
for the Arts
arts.gov

A&

OFFICE OF ARTS & CULTURE

SEATTLE

SEATTLE
FOUNDATION

WASHINGTON STATE
ARTS COMMISSION

Maureen Lee and Mark Busto
Rhoady Lee and Alan Gartenhaus
Ellie Mathews and Carl Youngmann as The North Press
Anne O'Donnell and John Phillips
Petunia Charitable Fund and advisor Elizabeth Hebert
Suzie Rapp and Mark Hamilton
Joseph C. Roberts
Jill and Bill Ruckelshaus
Cynthia Lovelace Sears and Frank Buxton
Kim and Jeff Seely
Catherine Eaton Skinner and David Skinner
Dan Waggoner
Austin Walters
Barbara and Charles Wright
The dedicated interns and faithful volunteers
of Copper Canyon Press

The Chinese character for poetry is made up of two parts: "word" and
"temple." It also serves as pressmark for Copper Canyon Press.

This book is set in Farnham, designed by Christian Schwartz. The
headings are set in Whitney, designed by Tobias Frere-Jones. Book
design by VJB/Scribe. Printed on archival-quality paper.

Printed in the USA
CPSIA information can be obtained
at www.ICGtesting.com
JSHW021959190324
59497JS00005B/16